RAGGED
ANTHEM

Made in Michigan Writers Series

General Editors

Michael Delp, Interlochen Center for the Arts
M. L. Liebler, Wayne State University

A complete listing of the books in this series can be found online at
wsupress.wayne.edu

RAGGED ANTHEM

Poems by Chris Dombrowski

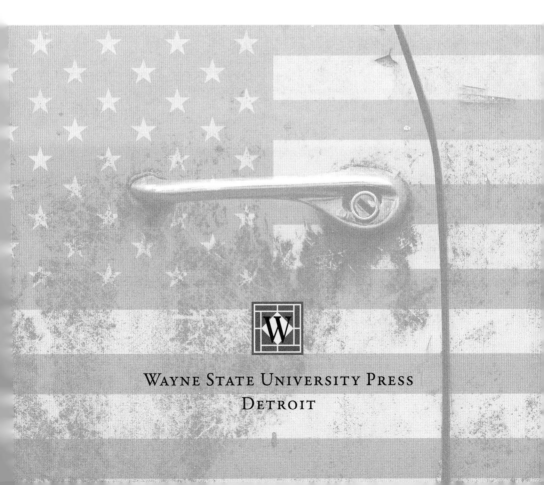

WAYNE STATE UNIVERSITY PRESS

DETROIT

This is a work of fiction. Any names, places, incidents, or characters resembling actual people, living or dead, is purely coincidental.

ISBN 978-0-8143-4653-2 (paperback)
ISBN 978-0-8143-4654-9 (e-book)

Library of Congress Control Number: 2018957220

Publication of this book was made possible by a generous gift from the Meijer Foundation. This work is supported in part by an award from the Michigan Council for Arts and Cultural Affairs.

michigan
council for
&arts
cultural
affairs

Wayne State University Press
Leonard N. Simons Building
4809 Woodward Avenue
Detroit, Michigan 48201–1309

Visit us online at wsupress.wayne.edu

CONTENTS

III.

I.

Imagination is that around which
    Mysteries assemble for devotion.

           —JAMES GALVIN

Gentle Reader

Gentle reader, I had to rent a room
for the few I paid toward would not suffice,

and upon its brown velour walls
tacked drawings my daughter'd made, around

the bed until they resembled a ring of stones
I stood inside or leaves a grove of aspens clutched

one gusty evening, late November. I played
Unaccompanied Suite for a Stolen Violin over and over

in my head until someone next door
punched the flimsy wall and, when I refused to lower

the volume, peered shyly through
the peephole. Noon, sky's shoulders slumped

with star burden, what we were doing
at noon in our respective rooms not up for discussion,

but we stood there, eye to glass-shrunk eye,
until one of us thought he saw the other's anger

flinch. Either that or a page,
despite the windows being shut, fluttered

like the wings of a lit bird
and we both of us turned to look.

I'm working on a building

The old man who swept his stoop each day
is sweeping still, the hardest-working motherfucker

in Motherfuckerville. At the door, your boyhood dog
greets you as the dust she is. You can't recall

her name. Drop your bag and lie down in the bed
you've longed for, your dreams most potent here.

If once there was a girl who lay with you, ignorant
of the tumor blooming beneath her brown hair,

she lies there still. Let her sleep. Don't act so smart
you come out sounding dumb, he said one morning

while scrambling eggs, or devolve into a milksop
whose life is background music to his thoughts,

and as for fools, suffer only yourself. These scraps
return with little else. A holiday or two. Merry

Christmas if you mean the one where Grandma
returned after the aneurysm, her unruly tongue falling

like a sad flag down her chin. Happy Easter, too,
whatever that implies. It could mean everything

here is just waking, stars in the skylight pitiless
but about to constellate. Mean practice, practice,

put your faith in that. The note you wrote yourself
on your Rawlings: *Get low, stay down on the ball.*

A density of quiet save the refrigerator that hums.
A stillness save the motes you've stirred. Listen,

the good dog at the back door is either whining or
you're crying to yourself. The start of a song.

Phrases

Boathouse sex—if you aren't aroused yet,
you'll never be. *Whiskey and branding irons*:
cringing, no? *Fresh bread* and the chakra
nearest the heart softens. I squirmed
and turned the music up when my son,
playfully torturing his friend, said *chew
on wet wool, chew on wet wool!* At nine
for me and Steve Sinadinos riding six
hours home from Peoria in grass-stained
jerseys, it was *panty hose*, the phrase
unstitching us with laughter, my mother
patient well past her threshold because
Steve's dad had died the month before
in the Dominican Republic, *business trip*
conjuring to this day the image of a man
facedown in a Santo Domingo swimming
pool. Years earlier he had run his sedan
off the dry highway, driving a fence rail
and neck tie through his sternum, later
gaining survivor's fame on Ripley's,
that life one of the several he spent,
his sister told me, on his way to the casket
I looked into thinking myself brave
as Steve and his cousins milled around
the punch bowl. Entrances, words,
doors cut deep in clay. I meant to say
something about the universality
of a phrase like *trembling winter grass
over snow*, but his aunt asked softly
did he want some macaroni? *Macaroni*,
he said. *Macaroni?* He laughed, spilling
punch. He split a side saying the word,
laughing as the rest of us wept.

Paperboy

A paperboy's fear of dogs: which unchained one
would charge, which lashed one
lope across the yard to the end of its singing links,
snap back yelping as he tossed the rag
rolled tight and rubberbanded toward the door,
metallic thump inside star-whirl
made audible by cicada chatter and early commuters,
August, a month that had lain beside
the industrial river and lost its virginity,
everything losing something, some point,

he would tell his son, decades later after a saccharine
pop song prompted the boy to ask about
his childhood dead. Were there any? Sure as moths
sleep with folded wings, Son. The boy's
subsequent silence: puff of breath the big moon was
on those cold October nights when her skin
at waistline was warmer than the womb. And the boy
wonders why, as we walk to school
past the Rott-mix lunging at the bent chain link,
I grasp so frantically for his hand.

Bird in My Boot

I have a bird in my muck boot, a leak
that collects water and squeaks with each
step. I thought to patch it but prefer

the company of an invisible warbler
who's quiet until I walk and goes with me
until I pause, perhaps a lark, can't tell,

its call muffled under footfalls, refugee
of the seraphim to be sure. *In a dark time*,
a poet born near my birthplace wrote,

the eye begins to see. He also knew how
to spell Tittabawassee and that it flowed
via the Saginaw into a desecrated bay

like the shining eyes of a drinker
dulling as a bottle drains. I'm not
refuting, only saying that the ear

begins to hear as well, mine did, slight
wings and their settling. I lived on a bay
I wished to enter permanently despite

a beloved's touch and the predawn
whisperings of our children in the room
adjacent, and took heart in the poet's

wondering if madness wasn't *nobility of soul*
at odds with circumstance until a young man
several states away, a child really, entered

a school and shot twenty children. I untacked
the quoted syllables from the wall. Madness
was madness, that's all. The wind that day

blew very hard and a kestrel hover-hunting
coastline snatched a woodcock from the air,
turning the late migrant into a formless

swirl of feathers, then stood in the yard
picking plumage from its prey's upturned
breast. Slick meat hanging from its beak,

it stared me down, masked eyes looking past
my human to the one that aches to survive—
it lit ultimately in a blur of gray-orange,

leaving its mark to billow as it disappeared
into that country owned by the winged,
upon whose constant intercession I depend.

The Turn

Fall's altering light on first snow veining
young granitic peaks. Magisterial.
It's too late to be a gathering of larch trees
two rainy days from turning, or too early,
but I can dream, can't I? One October
underwater near the mouth of a tributary
stream up which salmon made their way,
I swam listening to billions of sand grains
tick against each other, then surfaced
to a coho wearing the gravel redd, his fins
away. I was a creature once and want
again to relish a last apple from the branch
the way this backyard fawn does, forelegs
resting on trunk, hind hooves in the lawn.
Nearby, a boy stands at the bus stop, my son,
frost flaking from ditch grass onto his Nikes,
his breath before him, then swept
into the chrome grin of a passing sedan,
his backpack bulging with the history
project we finished at the breakfast table
that doubles as my desk. However fleet, time
stalls long enough for said vehicle to morph
from red Scion into my father's blue Skylark,
dropping me off three decades ago, duffle
weighed down with boy fears, chief
among them that he wouldn't return
to pick me up. How eternal the minutes
seemed when he was five, six, seven late,
the winter sun already slipping. I recall
much less of those other incarnations—
fish, doe, let alone mountain—I think,
as the school bus brakes without regard for
reverie, and hinging open its pressured door
reflects a sunrise the peak's high larches lord
momentarily above us, flashing me back to my
current appointment: squire of the light, our sire.

The Congressman's Daughter

That no one taught us
what species of tree
our No. 2 pencils
were made from could be
precisely the reason
we're warping to Hades
in a Hermes clutch
but we'll pardon her
as she had tests, four
standardized, to teach
to, Ms. Dolan, a bulldog
until the bubble forms
were filled, a graphite
mass of pupils, caught
me flushed one recess
in the janitor's closet
with June McKee, fairest
daughter of our House's
most distinguished
member, he rumored
to drink Irishly and
return from interns'
offices with shirttails
untucked—the desks
back then had basins,
doors that hinged like
coffin lids, the books
in this cumbersome
metaphor a vehicle
for what tenor? Her
pupils constricting

at the fluorescent light
as the kids from four-
square filed in, but Dolan
never called our folks,
casting her vote for
desire over order—
you can be so many
things in this world but
you can only be
so many things in this
world. I dig these snap-
shirts, their pearl buttons
clicking against the keys.

Geology Lesson

If I say *glacial lake*, you might think cold and slow,
but she left the way a woodcock leaves a grove
of poplars for a distant stand of ash, and I awoke

in the manner of one facing a firing squad, waves
pacing against the shore above which stars flared
too much like the muzzles of guns, indifferent wind,

hint of horizon like a querulous line of grief
in her voice, sky draining its dark the way a basin
lets go its lake and finds in its place a river lingering

like sweat fallen across earth's face. Once, nude,
she lay down on made sheets, then rose to smoke
a cigarette, the cotton embossed with her contours.

In this way the Bitterroots were formed.

First Hour

Wake up, get out of bed, feel the cold porcelain
on your bare ass, is what the cardinal says
each morning, my translation. Only once
this season has the bird shirked, a confounding
union break—who would open the door
holding back dawn, with what jangling key?

ꝑ

Up but hardly at 'em, I'm just a runt whimpering
at the whelping box's edge until mutely it arrives
carrying something I couldn't from somewhere
I've never been. Splinter of dawn through the glass
candle holder. Old friend unsure of whether
to shake hands or embrace: when did you get in?

ꝑ

Falling frost scales at daybreak. Who has eyes
let him see cold motes called back, vanishing
without dimple into the lake that washes under
its growing shelf of ice like a chorus of crickets
or night frogs, the gears of the universe turning
against each other. Who has ears let her hear.

ꝑ

The covey flushed past me towing with it wind
that made palpable though no more graspable
the vacancy between man and birds—sharptails—
as pearls of water slid down cattails into the slough,
sunlight sketching with nearly audible charcoal strokes
a surround, and I felt slight, but certain, comfort.

ꝑ

At a loss for the verb for when last night's wine
turns to a sugary alarm clock in the veins, I was
startled by Lily, who'd sprung her crib, climbed
with silent, enviable mettle the unlit stairwell
and snuggled in. Mid-January, waves breaking
against the ice. *Daddy, we can open presents now?*

♀

Camped at Priest Butte, I watched a doe chewing sage
push her wet nose past the tent flap, opening
the view to thousands of landing geese, snows
lit from below by the lake's roseate water.
Creatures with hollow bones whose burden
is light. Magdalene didn't visit the tomb at noon.

Bull Elk in October River

The elk was a boulder the Blackfoot flowed around,
spooked granite with tines and steaming nostrils, musk
the water wept away.
                    Reflection of honeysuckle gone to seed,
morphing, albinistic, stirred silt-like downstream.
                                        The light
smelled the way frost feels melting between two fingers
and a blade of grass.
                    Whatever'd harried the bull slinked
through the kinnikinnick, more fearsome, hidden, than it
had been bearing fangs.
                    I scanned the aspen trunks for fur,
scanned quaking shade through high-end optics, wagered
wolf duo pinning prey between banks, though it could have been
a cat, a camouflaged man in a stand.
                                In time the antlered
boulder walked ashore with dripping hide, its reflection
sinking, weightless as a worry, to the cobbles.
                                        My own worry
remained vague though it tracked me
through winter, constant as current, though I had no name
for it, perhaps because I had no name for it.

To the First of the Getting-Longer Days

I felt unsettled driving northeast in the dark
up what the Salish called the Road to the Buffalo
long before my tribe struck its camp of cul-de-sacs
though some still speak the Road's name in Salish,
further evidencing my aforementioned sense
of self-importance inherited from forefathers who also
wanted more and newer things such as cars without
fender dents that don't burn motor oil at a slow
if determined pace, such that checking the level
seems necessary every few hundred furlongs,
but then again I own it, even if the gasket job
cost roughly what the car was worth, and even
if I'd put repairs on a Visa—this line of thought
continuing as dawn stretched her blue shawl
over the Scapegoat, which is to say I felt the guilt
privilege affords and justly since I was driving
with my setter to hunt pheasants, chiefly a sporting
endeavor so removed from horseback and buffalo
jumps—the NPR station fizzled into white noise
and twenty miles from the next gas station I had to
relieve myself. What a flock of warblers was doing
so close to the mountains on the winter solstice
and chattering in the dark as the falling snow melted
flake by flake into my forehead, not even the most
learned ornithologist could have determined,
but they called assuredly from the sage as though
they had always been calling, and I finished
pissing, though perhaps I had always been pissing,
and men shouldering full quivers rode up the road,
one of them glancing to regard not traveler but song
as the light arrived, or kept arriving, as it will.

Like a December apiary, the mind tapers

to the subtlest hum in the year's dying light.
Wood smoke leans into the foothills, lingers.

That we possess no move as reconstituting
as the jowl-snapping headshake of a dog is clear.

The house lights flickering in the valley
buoy me, though, their being there at evening.

At a lecture I learned the mind of winter,
the emptied one, is privileged and classed.

Children bent over schoolwork, some broth, warm
kitchens against the dark like a mantleful of candles.

There is another world, Tweeted the visiting poet
while pointing to her screen, but it is in this one.

I imagine these kitchens, of course. It could be
worse, but no worse than our collective complicity.

While sitting by this river one windy afternoon
I heard a huge cottonwood bole start to split.

Enlightenment, said a monk, is failure after failure,
the blame, when only one is there, falling on oneself.

Swirling green cerebrum first, the tree plunged
into the water, knocking the wind out of the bottom.

I swear the valley held its breath. Then the first bird
pipped. But before that. Whatever that stillness was

I want no matter the offense. Tonight a cow elk
crosses, the sound of her hooves on cobbles

muted by current slurring into the distance. A breeze
plays the pop bottle of my empty shotgun barrel—

midstream, she swivels, ears keened.

The Hunt

The toothless milkmaid I'd mistakenly called sir,
upon whose land I'd asked to trespass, said her acres
were mine. Hoarfrost quiet. The Missions hidden
in a long lake deep cloud. The Flathead's blue bending
with a sense of ownership through the valley. A flush,
explosion of snow above the rosehips, a long shot missed.
Stopped to say a few words to the roots of an old willow
I'd met years ago, who was shy at first, what with my absence
and all. We touched as the pup pointed the ghost of a partridge
I once killed. A large covey's tracks led through Russian olive into
bull thistles and horizon held ample light, my game bag
mere feathers—but if I left now I could get Lily from preschool
just as the girl who told me her favorite color was *aquadarine*
awoke from her nap. Heel, boy. A doleful look from the kenneled
dog. Town's plowed streets were bright with melt, and inside
she slept beneath a purple blanket, a plush black bear gripped
in her left hand. In her mouth, fit tight, her right thumb:
a lone girl on a foldout mat on the classroom rug, the other kids
gone home. A nobleman went into a far country to obtain
for himself a kingdom and returned. Far from noble, I knelt
before her and let my kingdom sleep a while longer. Then spoke
softly, softly, to wake her from whose dream I could not say.

Cottonwoods

Through the coulee a river of cottonwoods runs.
In winter the river runs dry, all but a trickle.

But autumn the water's golden and its running
drowns out even the real river's running.

You can breathe inside this water, too, and let
its conflagration raze the brain's old homestead.

It's just yellow leaves, though, their stems' ends
aphid-bulbed, freckled and edged with brown.

A long time ago when God was reading the earth
the angels interrupted, pleading for another galaxy.

He made this stand his bookmark. Some frigid nights
you can almost hear the dusty spine unfolding.

Just a little green, like the nights when the northern lights perform

Indisputably I recognize the cumulus overhead
as a portion of the night sky the aurora borealis
illuminated years ago while I lay with Liz Charles
in the back of Toby Lawrence's Westfalia, petting

heavily until Lawrence appeared with a knock
on the hatchback, "The. Northern. Lights. Man,"
an indication he'd made little progress of his own
with the congressman's daughter in the uncut corn

so I removed my hand from the denim waistline,
the copper button of which I had just undone,
and stepped flushed into the breath-seizing night
under the red-and-green firmament billowing

like a gown of light, a mere ten miles from Lansing's
chained factory gates. Back at the party none could
fathom the kaleidoscopic heavens we described, nor
months later acknowledge what pulsed in Liz's

brain. Fainting spells soon forced us to, a shaved
head, its tidy box of stitches, a monthlong migraine
covered by ill-fitting wigs, hats. Then one evening
in June we sat on the sidewalk like kids and drew

with chalk. "I'm going to wherever they draw
on the sidewalk all day," she said. And soon did,
reappearing now and then to swim flirtatiously
through dreams before slipping the subconscious's

grip, so much like this white cloud that eludes
the branches' grasp before lofting west: the wind-
blown work of her hands—long-traveled, adrift
from parts celestial, a word I haven't quite relinquished.

Going Home

There must be rivers there—if there is a there
to which we depart, or, as some say, *return*,

rivers strewn with moonlight and discarded
shopping carts, mouths of springs choked

with forget-me-nots, long-slavering rills
threading rusted culvert grates, rivulets

splitting thickets, and boulder-curled cataracts
pocked by sewers pissing virulent strains of Time—

I've imagined them: all of the earth's rivers
moving at once. I think we'll need them and forever.

℘

In the Grand, they found Leon Stockwood's
body, but it wasn't till they looked upstream

that they found his head, in the Red Cedar, Sewer,
as we boys called it. Aroused by the blockbusters

his well-coiffed Hollywood stepdad made,
we pined all winter for the heated pool inside

their house, a chlorinated waterfall spilling into
the shallow end, always the sound of water,

tall windows steaming from floor to ceiling
as we'd move in and out of the mist.

℘

Let's say they let me in and allowed me take
one river, I know what mine would be, namelessly

unspooling through a Northwoods cedar bog,
its currents as soft as my daughter's foot wrapped

in her ballet slipper, a small braid of mayflies
rafting down, drab yellow, two shades paler

than the mayapple in early bloom,
or say they said I could enter but couldn't

bring my river, or could stay and stay the grass
draped along its banks: I guess I'd stay the grass.

♀

You can't cry in a river. At least they can't prove
you did. Autopsy said they drowned him before

they sawed his neck from his torso. Separate bags:
black and zipped and cast like Jitterbugs we raked

across those eddies. Crawdads worrying at his
whitened skin about the time the newspaper

reported he'd gotten "in over his head." I only played
JV with him, Frenched his sister when she relented,

but reckon he wouldn't have shed a tear—not a
drop that would've added to the current's push.

♀

What is it in me—or who—insists that proverbially
rowing across the river is somehow richer

than a sprig of mint broken near my nose, more
alluring than a sandy mouthful of cress or my son

descending the switchbacks with his headlamp on.
That river? Two black wolves crossed the Boulder

below a bend I fished, shook dry, then flowed
up the tawny sidehill and loped downcountry,

calling through a warm fall wind to one another
or to others on the far bank they could not see.

❡

Two black wolves. I heard their musculature
resist the water, then saw sunlight bristling

off their coats. In this world it came to pass.
Did you ever see a wolf, Leon Ward Stockwood,

my dear Liz Charles into whose skull surgeons
sawed, Asa Bromley clutching the wheel

as your Suburban rolls over in Iowa? A gymnasium
full of crying teens. The basketball team sitting

arm in arm, Leon whispering to me, *The fuck.*
He's gone. No goddamn song'll bring him back.

❡

That winter I watched the Red Cedar's currents
burbling under tiers of ice, constellations of frost,

occasional fish-glint—but I bent toward that
which I could hear, ear pressed as if

to a pulse. *You're carrying something?*
How far has it come? Muffled answers

issued forth that only a drowner
could distinguish. I stepped back from the shore.

If colors are indeed the works and sufferings
of light, I reckon water's must be sound.

                    ♀

Chairperson, Members of the Coalition
against the Thoreauvian Notion of Time,

I implore you to consider my great-grandfather
soaped and stripped to his suspendered drawers

in the Detroit River, holding my father's hands,
the boy swinging in the faint current like a kite

lagging on its string, or an eyelash about to be
tugged free. Not yet wished upon. Detroit River

full of duck shit and blood, gasping carp
and holographic oil. Windsor on the other side.

                    ♀

Covered in quilts, in a room without furniture
save the straight-back in which he sat,

my father's father, as far down as one can climb
into the drink, to whom I'd been brought

to say good-bye, though I'd never said hello. That
he'd abandoned his three children, I knew, but

I hoped for some last gesture beyond a handshake,
begged my father, who I'd never seen so staunch.

Could I have been that gesture? St. Christopher,
protect him. Ferry him if you have the oars.

                    ♀

My father and I drove to the pier afterward,
gazed in a silence the river wrapped itself around,

Archie Shepp's "Going Home" playing
from the grainy cassette deck—

that flourish after Parlan's fingers
fall spent on the piano keys, a final

exhalation in which the sax is purged of sound,
a stream's last riffle finishing brightly

at the mouth in the bay, resting place
of breath toward which the water ushers.

II.

On the walls of a dark room
    Where the world used to be
    Everybody's famous, everybody's free.
    Everybody's broken heart is shining like a new TV.

—JEFFREY FOUCAULT

Statesboro Blues

You've got three minutes
to say what you want to say. Beyond that
no one hears a thing. So what
if there's the epic denouement of a monarchy
to detail, just say: There's a moon,
a boy walking, somebody crying. The rest of us
trying to mainline darkness
from the Little Dipper's spoon. *Wake up, Mama,*
turn your lamp down low. From bed
two lovers lean up to dress though they've had all
they'll get of that. And this is the jags,
true as a dog's dick is red, this is the hour before
the blue hour, the tattered hour
when the moths arrive to darn the firmament
lest all the light leak out at dawn—
don't worry. There'll be birdsong soon.

Inauguration

Starlight in the icicles. A week so cold
even the freshest deer droppings fail
to melt the snow. To the flickering *h*
in the Thunderbird Motel's red neon
we endow a theosophical meaning
but explications lead to unheated
debate. In the hatband of the cowboy
in front of me in this listless line is stuck
a toothpick. Used, but that's recycling
in the New West. Brim tipped, he pays
the clerk with a silver dollar so worn
the face of—who was it?—is as faint
as the memory of weightlessness
in the womb.

Poem in which Morgan Freeman Narrates the Apocalypse

As many ways to get to Heaven
as to the pharmacy. Aborted
baby. Suicide bomb. The leper's
feet, when washed, appeared
skinless. Soiled, grandmother
needs her bedclothes changed
again. On the schoolyard a boy
bounces a half-flat basketball,
the worn rubber rising almost
to his hand. Tending this pulse
he is one of the seven beings
holding Earth in orbit or he is
tardy for class. Likewise a syringe
shining beneath the hoop, left
by a man who's very high if he isn't
scrambling to prep an IV
for his wife who declined to wear
her blond wig today. Pockets emptied
he stands stymied as the ball,
lofted toward the hoop, rattles
chain-link net—but swish
or air ball, it's hard to tell from here.

Was it a sign? I think it probably was

If the scantly visible braid of curlews
banking above the snowfield is a bracelet

adorning the land's pale wrist, can the northerly
charging down from Saskatchewan simply be

the wind, detached as an eye-doctor examining
retinas all day? It wearies one, the visionary mode,

pondering whether fog hovering above the creek
is a horde of souls about to descend, or a flock

of the same ready to lift. In the harsh light
of the optometrist's I thought my eyeball

with its thin red creeks and rivulets
looked like a delta viewed from elevation,

myriad rivers spilling into the pupil's
black ocean, but of course I was merely dilated,

vowing in the reclined chair to someday see
the world as the world, not a caption on my life—

but not this thawing February afternoon
in which I find, in a roadside puddle fringed with ice,

a male robin belly-up dead,
the earthworm in its beak still squirming.

Fig

Then, right there, smack in the middle of winter,
a fig from Marrakesh on the sample tray, February's
cold rain shading to sleet ticking against the windows,

February having seeped into bloodstreams, silent
as a pesticide through fruit skin. *But it says organic?*
O poet laureate of boot slush, the snow outside

is strobing, a density of white the air seems
reluctant to receive, clemency mere myth
if not stored within the gritty sugars of this fig,

offered now on a palm covered by plastic glove.
Biodegradable of course. A gesture only unabashed
pleasure can redeem. February, coy ash spreader,

leave our foreheads alone, we've enough reminders
of the dust to which we shall return. Take and eat.
Swirling outside the window a flurry of cherubs

waits to gauge the density of your joy. Reports to the Lord.

They Knew Each Leaf Contained
the Rain and Sun

Two girls read their poems under trees.
Really they were women but reading
they were girls conversing with magpies
and the thin-limbed aspens. Sky's a blue stone,
one of them told the other, held by
who knows whom. You look like death
on a cracker, the other told the other.
Regarding the mail, it won't come till yesterday;
it already arrived tomorrow. Stand me a drink,
then, a last unblinking look? And so on. They wore
white dresses that glowed in the half light
long after the west winked out. They allowed
the wind its interludes. If you were a wounded
bird they breathed into your beak until your wings
worked, if you were flitting busily they felled you
with polished stones. One said: I do not know
who wrote these. The other: I take back
everything I said, except that bit about your hands.

Hold me closer, tiny dancer

It was the day after the Banal Days Festival
and Frank was feeling a little exhausted,
hungover in this country full of heroes he was
indifferent to. He was trying to tell his son
they were rich because they owned two vehicles,
a 2002 Subaru with 106K, in good shape save
rusted side panels, and a '96 Toyota pickup,
but Frank Jr. was having none of it: Grady's dad
drives an Escalade and his mom's Volvo has
heated leather seats that just about jack you off—
Watch it! Frank yelled, wondering what such seats
would cost. A foul mouth gets mouthwash
all the way to the morgue, he said. Who's going
to the morgue? Frank Jr. asked. Who's not? We are
but farts in a matchbox, midwestern seers
shunned by their fellow townies. Frank Jr.
said he recognized this quip as what his teacher
called allusion, but to what he couldn't exactly
say. You know they dislike lesbians on Lesbos,
he said, cribbing from something he heard
on Sorority Girls Gone Wild. That island
gets far too much publicity. Your mom and I
owned a time share there for a year but I just
couldn't get ahead. Ahead of what? Ahead of—
Frank sat down on the curb next to a slug
someone's midnight shoe sole was bound
to squash into oblivion and sighed a fatherly
sigh, equal parts exasperation and anomie.
Look, I'm supposed to wipe my forehead
of sweat here and say something formative,
but all I can gather is that if you find yourself
singing along buzzed to "Tiny Dancer" and fail
to go falsetto on the chorus, you might have

lost your soul, capital S, or even worse be one
who disputes the soul's existence. He reached
into his wallet for a Visa card with which
he deftly peeled the slug from cement. Go forth
and toss that little guy into the trees, will you,
then pay yourself for your time at the sushi
stand. You are a Caucasian American male,
at fault for most of our nation's failings, at least
you can smother your already smothered guilt
with calories. He watched Frank Jr. shrug and make
for the mall's faux palms, then shuddered at
a memory of the boy in the baby carrier, tiny back
pressed against his chest, little arms reaching, legs
kicking a second heartbeat, occasional glee
shooting through the boy's frame and into
his own? O Father who invented time, for which
you are loathed, was I ever that small and if so—

I went down, down, down

Nose, nipple, belly button, ear, tongue ring,
cock ring, eyelid ring, wedding ring, engagement,
chastity, class ring, championship, plastic
bought for a quarter in the supermarket foyer
studded with a candy ruby sucked on
for a minute before dropping to the parking lot spills
of oil and antifreeze. *You can't have it now,
I'll get you another next time.* Dinner bell (who alive's
heard an earnest one?), boxing ring (square)
on which lies a portion of the champ's ear bitten off
by the much-maligned former champ,
telephone ring preceding a prerecorded infomercial
for debt consolidation, hangover headache
ring preceded by Meredith's money-doubling pours
and "Ring of Fire" chosen repeatedly
on the digital jukebox by the cattlehand's date
(*That's my girl!* he'd say with a rump slap)
grime rings in the toilet bowl (regarding urinals
do you pick the short one or the tall one
and will you urinate in one left unflushed? Well,
sure, who hasn't, but I once saw a tampon
in the freshwater pond, a miniature father and son
fishing for it from the pink disinfecting
puck so intently they weren't saying word one
to each other) like tide-lines, eons old
in the sandstone outcropping behind the mall.

It's so hard to dance that way, when it's cold and there's no music

It's a blustery, big-moon,
kiss-my-ass-if-you-thought-spring-was-coming
kind of morning but she's
running in it anyway, with grips called Yaktrax
strapped to her shoes despite yak
being largely herd walkers not known for speed,
though I digress while reclining fireside
with the predawn malarkey that often passes
for thought as I scroll through her
forgotten iPod loaded with albums released largely
when I was easier to love. With luck
the day will rotate toward one of those hoarfrosted
afternoons when a southerly sun
breaks the inversion and slight winds loose
tiny flakes of frozen frost-skin
from the branches and marble-hard ash berries
that the waxwings, long away, arrive
to love, their forms braced by laden branches
that settle briefly if at all before some
unnamed fear stirs the birds and the tree explodes
with the shrapnel of the miraculous—
but for now: the impossibly slow snare-drum count
of her steps against the ice I didn't
salt, careful steps, and she's back and letting inside
a cold that has rendered my cheek
somehow kissable—I scent the dark air's bristling
as her cheek brushes mine and she
strides away humming something, little exhumer,
that, note by spadeful note, unearths me.

Lunar Calendar

Three moons in particular appear to have it in for me:

The Moon of It Gets Late Early Here;
The Moon of Winter Stores Wearing Thin;
and The Moon of I Have to Quit Fishing and Return
Underappreciated and Underpaid to Work.

Of course there is also The Moon of Too Many
Plastic Presents and Cups of Unspiked Nog,
not to mention The Moon of Everybody But Me
Flies to a Beach Town and Drinks Free Margaritas;

And while I take rare comfort in The Moon of We Start
Anyway to Get Some Color Back in Our Cheeks,
it often devolves into The Moon of Crunching
Numbers for the Man.

Praise be, though, to The Moon of the Long
Larch-Colored Light! Unless of course you are
an herbivorian ungulate in which case it becomes
The Moon of Dodging Hurtling Pieces of Lead.
Moon of Not Too Much But a Little More Light Each Day,
I thank you and beg you not to morph into The Moon
That Recalls the Time She Left For Good; this goes
as well for The Moon of Picking Wild Asparagus,

which doubles as The Moon of When I Caught Her
in the Backyard Kissing Him, aka The Moon
of When All Resentment Ripens. But, Moon of
We Finally Put Our Fleece on Again and Watch You

Refracting Light onto the Peaks' First Dusting,
you redeem all other god-cast stones, as do you,
Moon of When the Muddy Water Clears and Trout
Can See My Flies Again—which leaves just you,

Moon of Wool Hats at Night but Naked Lake Swims
at Noon, Moon of Ripe Huckleberries by the Fistful,
Moon of Dragonflies Cupped in Daughter's Palms,
Moon of Everything (Even Talking to a Mute Stone) Is Alright.

Dept. Meeting

Listening to the speaker—disclosure, she said, consequence—
he could literally hear his soul

withering—sound of a swallowtail smashed midflight
frying on the semitruck's chrome grill—

which was fine because prior to this the soul's existence had seemed
disputable, but now—objectives, goal-based

outcomes, interdepartmental checks and balances—
he was certain he could feel

yellow wings adorned with dark whorls folding open,
fanning abandoned coals inside his chest,

smoldering away decades of academic bleating, vague
apolitical sterilization—and even if

this sensation were mere delusion, heartburn hallucination
brought on by faux-crab dip

catered by a food service staff under budgetary restrictions,
he vowed to view it as visitation: contact

with the actual, scant but inimitable wind that was suddenly
the only thing he heard.

I Text Jeffrey:

500 snow geese
300 yards from shore.

He texts back:
Good poem.

Stick fire, I text,
fog eliding long horizon.

A Rothko, he responds,
and free.

Calls somewhere between
a bellow and a yip.

Somewhere between?
Then where?

Out where land's
impossibly faint.

Then nothing more
from Jeffrey.

Though I fancied
the last line my best.

Windless dusk. I wait
for my pocket to vibrate.

Shore Song

I'm trying to be a lake or pond or even the water
gathered in the trough of the swale but most days
I'm just a teacupful, cooling far too quickly,
suddenly red when the rose petals curl and steep,
scalding when microwaved a minute. All night
the eaves did their weeping and this crisp dawn
they gnash their teeth, one of which on tiptoe
I remove: icicle slick with sunlight pitched
into the waves, an offering that will be subsumed
within the hour, barely noticed by the bay.

Midwesterly

I followed a braid of cabbage whites
past seas of east-facing swaying sunflowers
to reach this hardwood stand in Minnesota
just west of the Owl Café and Travel Plaza
inside which the mayo bottle's flatulence
rescued me momentarily from my penchant
for the pastoral. By any road-shoulder math
it's been a bad week for skunks, the shortcut
across the not-so-proverbial asphalt river
fatally short. How about the quickest route
to Hibbing? It's a horse apiece, the trucker
said, six of one, and cautioned strongly
against the Pizza Burger. Anywhere nearby
to take the edge off? I asked the ginger
waitress who said the crickets have curfews
around here. What brings you through anyway?
she asked. I shook the plastic saltcellar, said
work. She chuckled, set down the check.
As we both know, women are the reason
for everything, right? Peppermint on top.

Little Derivative and Forgivable Anthropomorphism with Dawn

On the porch in the sun reading M's poems
when a robin arrives toting a little something

for her pining fledglings, who stretch bald necks
toward that which they can't yet see. Rigidly,

above the tiny ruckus, from one side of her head,
she is sentry a good while, two or three poems—

the one where sunlight reflects from the blue
swimming pool onto the blue ceiling, the one

where the wind's a mixture of linen and salt—
before the worm's divvied into those fragile

orange bowls, and the fledglings hush. Is she,
despite instinct, affording me the morsel's worth

of the trust I sense? My grandmother wouldn't pass
until my mother, four days at bedside, slipped out

for a change of clothes, departing the way
our dead return: once we've stopped attending them.

Larches

We thin out like October larches,
born as we were to say good-bye

to the strange species of light
endemic to our valleys. Hosanna-

shouts, come-cries, froths of rage
spit skyward, our cadmium needles

scatter and the wind has its way
with them. By and by black granite

cups the shed: maybe a halo's worth
around the base of each rough trunk.

Hear them all

—*Wilma Theatre, Missoula, MT*

Dave Rawlings's Olympic archtop Epiphone
bucks like a cat on the livest of wires,

but at the moment of peak voltage, instead of
letting the thing leap high-haired from his hands,

the picker fixes his grip, a current snapping
through his lank frame, and like to spark. A man

with dreadlocks and a second man swaying
atop his shoulders move stageward, threading

other dancing bodies as Rawlings's reedy tenor
reaches *the lowliest who gather in their stalls,*

conjuring my grandmother's last hour, morphine,
Ativan, the night nurse on a break, and I wonder

what the phrase evokes for others moving
individually to the same notes I move to. Another

regards me from across the crowd—I know him
from his days on that television show where

the wannabes try out for the has-beens
who were mostly no good to begin with, but this guy

with his splintered Martin and rusted mouth harp
had a bona fide thing and was thus voted second,

soon after which I met him in a loud bar and began
to chat up his modestly burning fame-fire,

how best to stoke it, until he said, Frankly,
the shit I'm playing's bruised as a felled pear

buzzed by fruit flies, and explained with aplomb
that an order of beings was likewise assigned

to attend our rawest wounds, and used
the phrase returned to eternity before adding

that he had just seen Gillian and Dave at LA's
Aladdin and hadn't quite recovered, and had I

heard their new album, Time (The Revelator)—
Hasn't left my stereo, I said, and we clinked glasses

oblivious to the fact that the actual hour's turning
made it "Ruination Day," the record's sleeper tune,

and I walked home later through a cold April rain
huddled over the red coal of his words—the memory

of which makes me want to buy him a Makers'
recalled infallibly as his fancy, but the crowd's

stage-bound wave carries him with it, as Rawlings
warbles about *flowers growing in the rubble*

of the towers, and *the tenderest words from Zion,*
Noah's waterfall, his ragged anthem a wind

that stirs the torn tickets we are and lifts
the dreadlocked man, handsome companion

yoked upon his shoulders, who leans his stout
frame against the stage and opens his brown arms

as *the prophets from Elijah to the old Paiute Wovoka*
take their places at the table when they're called,

then with a yelp raises his face to the crowd, one tear
falling down his face like a bright stripe on an old flag.

Poem in Which I Lose My Wish to Drown

Once again Rothko's ghost
demands to inhabit my body: a gust
smacked against my ribs
though the bay's sheer all the way to Wisconsin,
a silver swelling horizontally to join
the vertical salmon flesh of dusk, horizon
keen as the slice I make with the tip
of this black old knife up the boated hen's
pale belly, her flanks falling open,
cavity spilling roe onto the boat's white floor
until I sense what he desired: the eggs'
orange translucence for his brush, this rank
muck upon his hands. Wave-slosh
sent from a far-off ferry. This voice calling *mine*
to carry, then melt into a blue he invented:
god that he was, I lord it over him and the gone.

III.

What's the name they call ones like us?
    A bouquet of shadows in the evening sun.

—RICHARD BUCKNER

Early June, Missoula, Year of the Sheep

High in the setting west, due south
of Venus seated brightly atop a waxing crescent,

floats Jupiter: sky's spheres rearranged
sufficiently so that the gone might pass through

as they wish, and excuse our doings
for a night or two. Pear tree in blossom,

in gusts that rend, musk of two
blooming lilacs, one white, one violet, mingling

as they set out. Try no matter what
sort of maelstrom to write one single clear line

in a notebook every day, said the sad
poet to his son, who would himself become

a sad poet. God pares a fingernail,
flicks it from his calloused palm and we muse

awhile about the moon, is a line
the son might have written but didn't. O you

who break us like the bottle
in which you hold our tears before sweeping

the shards skyward, yours is a perilous
radiance, about which the single passerine grasping

the beetle-ridden spruce above us
is more equipped to speak. Windy flames,

beloveds, the small flowers shift
through one another, the density of their married

scent deepening beyond the yard,
invisible offering issuing how far forth?

Boy with Tree Frog

He caught the singer in his hands before it sang,
slick, jumping-like-a-pulse thing in the small cave
his palms made, pliable, bird-boned, blinking other

before it could join the bark-hugging horde
that issued, call by call, day's dirge, issued evening,
dusk, a focalized riot of geese calls, then dark

and the susurrus of cupped wing tips cutting water,
a moon above detangling itself from pines, its light
like spilled scales across the lake, like the liquid

incarnation of a god whose first commandment is
release: and so he did, the little live thing. Back into
a world that begs to be breathed, not remembered.

Saying Moon in Dusk

Good Harbor, MI

The mating pair of salmon washed ashore
at Shalda's mouth—they do not praise,

as I too often do, the austere, but they
inarguably are: the buck's white teeth

blanching in moonlight as its swart flanks
darken on wet sand, the hen's eye socket

picked clean by gulls that must have hoisted
the vitreous skyward and left it hanging,

hence the gibbous. Or so I tell my daughter,
year-old and walking shoreline with me, saying

for the first time in her short life the word
moon: which silvers the water cape to cape

as it swims the long miles from her mouth
to the radiant place where it was born.

Francis

A friend brought me stones from Assisi,
Convento Dei Capuccini where Francis walked.

They sit on my sill in a burlap sack
closed tight by rope like a robe's belt.

Seven stones plain as pea-gravel,
small worn portions of the earth.

I was told to handle them only under
duress, and naturally I do so daily.

In the dark before the birds who preferred
his shoulders to branches begin to sing.

I am no monk, though, no eater of ashes
excepting the remnants of anger on my tongue.

Trying to pray, I often fall asleep, the case
again today, the stones sweaty in my palm

as I dreamed a statue of Francis, the kind
that frequents gardens, had fallen from a stoop.

Lichen grew bright green upon its brow,
and gone-to-seed dandelions blanketed its legs.

Clutching at her stomach, a young woman
walked forlorn down the evening street.

High lamps flickering, it had just rained,
perhaps Detroit, but something said Portland.

Through chain link, the woman's palpable
anguish pried open the statue's stony eyes.

What happened next, I feel stirred to say,
was dream, not writing, not me writing now.

The statue stood and became a man, rock
reconstituted as flesh, with a female face.

Robed, hooded, scurrying from yard
to porch, calling birds to hand, small dog

to its side. Then seizing again into stone
in time for the walker to glance up and see

a swirl of beckoned sparrows alight
on the statue's steady head. The woman,

from underneath her bolt of brown hair,
drew a finger across her brow, looked up.

Why myth not skin, I wondered, waking,
slipping the stones back into their sack.

When a kiss on the hand, a fistful of bills
seemed plausible. Within the realm.

Or is the flesh sometimes too frightening
to help? In my own palm this morning

my nails left indentations, as if invisible birds
had landed, fed on scattered seed, and lit.

Swallows Building Nests

When I am mud let me be
the woman whose bust the swallows
sculpt tonight beneath
barn eaves, whose breasts they duck
iridescently into, bright
tongues into self-made mouths, wings
of caddis twitching briefly
between beaks. Whose nape and stooped
shoulders they shape with
unstudied abandon. A wonder: will they
drop the daub of me stolen
from wasps or rear back to regard
my scant role in the form,
the love of which is a love of endings,
of which I know better. Though
who wouldn't wish for one into which
small birds will fold.

Swale

If it isn't the prettiest word
in the language, tell me what is—

the *S* a blue racer's disappearance
making secret the place; the lips

squinched, poised at the *W*;
then parting—the way in—before

the tongue lands lightly on grass,
wet, as it was when I was a child,

when I spoke as a child if mostly
to myself surrounded by stems bent

by their seeds, a poised wave
cresting green and the shade it cast

cooling the trough of what I called
a ditch. My father taught me

the proper word, a hint of which
I hear as my daughter insists

she's a *big gale* and should be allowed
to travel to the hospice bed with me—

my father whose mouth will open
a few more times to say he's not hungry—

a wind, indeed, what a strong gust
you are, I say, but her face reddens—

No, she stomps, *big gale!* The young
tongue's way, I see, of saying *girl.*

Brook Trout

For eons light survived underwater, trapped
in white-rimmed fins finally held forth
by a boy's small hands, the villagers squinting
as if it were the Arkenstone or each onlooker's
single deepest sorrow unremarked upon for decades,
and when they asked how he had come to catch it
with its back caped in grayish trails,
he answered, on worms his sister dug by sound.

April Ghost Sonnet

How many rainy afternoons have I
fallen asleep while reading a poem,

book spine up on my chest. Not enough
if you ask one recently awoken

from such an occasion, recto and verso
rising and falling like lungs filled

with another's breath, another's lines
like black ribs fitted neatly beneath

my own. Sweet soil, that slight but certain
weight. And the first flower of sentience

blooming, before all of this, like the purple
blackberry-shaped one I picked for you

years ago, juice can for a vase, the dear
one, dewy, whose name I still don't know.

Nuptials

Love is the first line, a fruit
found on the ground, and a marriage
the forming of the tree from which the fruit
grows, or so said Valéry regarding poems.

We were in Chile for a week, my love and I,
a honeymoon fifteen years in the wings.

I say *my love,* but if you knew a wrinkle's worth
of the rotting mastodon carcass of things
I've said and done, you'd ask me to, please,
use another term of endearment.

And yet: I love her, and we were there, under
condors, giant ibis, green flocks of parakeets.

Where spring water burbled from a cliff
we drank. A fox leapt to watch her wade
a lupine meadow, leapt head high,
then disappeared into a wave of blooms.

We bought two trail-dusted hitchhikers *tortas*
for lunch. Salmon, they were starved
for salmon. Drove to the pass as they shared bites
in the bed of the pickup, folded leftovers into foil.

Snowfield and cloudshadow.

To a *huaso* who let us trespass a cold river winding
through his land we offered three beers. And honey.

I'm going to keep walking in the world this way,
whatever and wherever that way may be,
I wrote in my journal while she bathed and sipped
lemon tea, and though I've tried, I haven't much.

How young that Virgin looked on the church's mural,
our breath fogging the window, our reflections.

New Year's we danced at Piedro Rojo, a brothel
turned discotheque, the flashy young men navigating
through smoke and bass-thump to gyrate near her,
a *gringa* who for a few moments owned the floor.

If I had knelt down with a new ring and asked
she would have said maybe, probably, not no.

We vowed to carry new rituals into our days,
to wake and touch one another before opening
ourselves like petals from a flower the good children
pick. To drink tea. Forgave, in advance, our failures.

Late one fishless windy day, she asked the river
for a trout; momentarily: a four-pound brown.

On a borrowed guitar, in a stranger's wind-buffeted
casita, she sang—*You pass through places, and places
pass through you, but you carry them with you on the soles
of your traveling shoes.* Chicken stew on the woodstove.

Her lithe voice constellated, bright as the Southern Cross
shining like root-light piercing dark loam, our tree's new soil.

The littlest birds sing the prettiest songs, the littlest birds . . .
The broth chock-full of celery, onions, lentils, bones.
Walking late that evening we spooked a fledgling
quail. It hovered and fell into the tall grass. Sudden as a plum.

Grove

Root, bole, branch, stem, leaf: wavering
in wind's stringencies. Of spider webs,
one spindrift trails its spinner and cache
of snakefly captives. Fellow travelers,
what does the land require of us? Lie down
in an October grove, stand after a spell
and walk away without looking back
on your leaf-stenciled shape, gilded grass,
as the snow goose sees it, the migratory snipe,
and soon—north gust or not—the aspens
have quilted you in. Day's great seed
flowering, as light quits the meadow,
all at once: You, once banished, again belong.

Another rapture rescheduled,

the fey preacher's prophecy
a prophecy not so much. I walk
the dry wash for morels, blond
caddis ovipositing on the cobbles
where recently the river ran, where
it will run again, provided. Again
I took daybreak for granted, easy
as mistaking pinecone for wasp nest,
wasp nest for shed antler, antler
for branch. Wrongly I read the earth
as a text that has been penned
rather than something that is being
written—this pocketed fork-horn
simply a buck's early draft, scorings
at its base a sure sign the porcupine
found it first. From his knees my son
once discovered in a ponderosa's
rooted warrens a litter of rabbits
slick-skinned and shivering together,
and another time, through a squint
in a mission's door, a painting of Jesus
gilded and presiding over a supper
someone named the last. I asked
the four-year-old if he wanted the door
unlocked but he remained rapt,
peering through the eyelet as pews
darkened, evening closed. He stepped
suddenly back, his thick eyebrows
arced as if the painting had—what?—
winked. No explanation requested,
and none today as I find, protruding
from matted grass, in a boot track
I left an hour ago, the first morel:
whorled thumbprint of a god.

Just Before Dark

The creek water has a way with the light
and the light a way with the water,

both having come from so far to get here
to morph away in an instant above cobbles

birthed millenniums ago by mountains
that are rising even as they recede:

facts so believable this August evening
as the front drags behind the peaks a tablet

of welt-blue sky. Upstream a man is dying
but who isn't he would ask, his tan old face

canyoned, gullied, a map in high relief
or a heart halved and drained of that other

liquid we can't live without. Downstream,
poured from my glass, a gout of wine

blooms in the clear flow before vanishing
in the cacophonous gossip of currents—

it was rumored but now doubtless that the light
and water were lovers, and this earth the endless

bed on which they consummate. Making us
their children: orphaned here awhile, adrift

in the radiant air before they return
to claim us, saying again our original name.

The unwritable girl

May snowmelt glides
toward greening prairie
over which two harriers
scribe their arcs. Current
shackling his ankles,
a man stands watching
his six-year-old daughter
pick still-moist morels
from shoreline grasses
shaded by cottonwoods
whose tacky blooms exude
the scent upon which
his faith is based. Wind,
the wind blows warmer,
spilling the harriers
downcountry as the girl
glancing into her sack
uses the word *crestfallen*
in unaffected speech:
as in, if she hadn't found
any morels this morning,
she'd've been.

Coda

Under a winter's worth of melting snow,
Swan Lake is a fresh sheet of rice paper

and the half-sunk round of larch
charred from an ice fisherman's fire

the precise place the Great Poet
rested her ink-wet brush momentarily

before raising it and abandoning
the poem for the view.

Cooking Christmas Dinner with My Son, the Runner

I batter the halibut I traded elk steaks for, drip
leftover egg into the pan, scrambling a present
I slide into the dog's steel bowl. Brussels
halved and oiled I let loudly fall into a skillet
congealed with bacon grease. In the garage,
curing, hangs yesterday's harvest, a pheasant
from which I ask Luca to carve four portions
with the knife he unwrapped today, "Just
breasts and legs, we'll skin the rest tomorrow,
make stock for soup." I stir as the setter
that pointed the bird in Russian olives, fetched it
from cattails, sits tall, sloppily licking his chops
before splashing elegantly to the opening door
where Luca proffers the meat. "Dad," he says,
staring at two pink breasts on the cold white plate,
"I'm sorry. But as a runner I cannot cut the legs
from another animal," a teaching, I reckon—
popping a hot Brussels into my mouth, chewing,
releasing the steam—that must be pursued
far beyond the limits of pursuit.

Like a pearl in a sea of liquid jade

When Jesus had come halfway across
the glistening bay, he saw in the looming
squall a dense vacancy, stern as a father's
blind eye, and thought of turning back
though their sad nets beaded with evening
beckoned him, their bickering skipping
across waves made of breath. The bay's
scent, a mother's neck folds known
precisely by her nursing child, thrust him
into a reverie so fierce he recalled a future
very distant and a poet arrogant enough
to write a few lines from his view, as Peter
came flailing over the hull obliterating
the vision. The next step tests, but what?
he asked, knowing Peter took his footfalls
as some trick of light, of subtle elevation.
Later much was made of the storm, which
truth be told, and it must, was mostly virga
and heat lightning giving way to dark sky,
to stars cast like sand grains on becalmed
water: strange constellation tracing his steps.

See that my grave is swept clean

Out here I can see what God's got going, I can love a single tree.
The storm-front
levitating off the ridgespine is a twenty-mile-long Rothko, the canvas on loan
from Gabriel.
Duff sail, a swath of ancient light falls instantly from the clouds,
recalling a phrase my daughter whispered, her eyes: two tears choked back.
The grass
in which I lie is timothy, the chin in my palms mine as I watch the slipping sun like a
child prone before a fireside nativity.
Green flash like those seen above the sea,
though who's sailing, and who's an anchor plummeting geologically through grass
remains unearthed.
Time, then, it would appear, to study a slug, faceless, mistaken
for a catkin, wind with whom the aspens nicker.
The tendencies of frost.
To ponder
the works of gods as opposed to those of angels, as opposed to the green eternity of
this Russian olive, and the sound she's making in the breeze.

Tablet

To obey, wake in the dark and put your head
in your hands. Look out the window and rest
your cheek on the shoulder of the mountain.
Rise and walk to where the creek falls finally
into the river—there an apple tree stands hung
with one last fruit: pick it, or if it hangs too high
knock it down with a branch and eat it in three
juice-spilling bites. From your knees kiss
the rill surrounded by forget-me-nots, beckon
a brook trout to your hands, and if one arrives
study the vermiculate script worming along
its sides. Over a stick fire cook the fish until
its skin pales and peels back from the orange
flesh, then feed yourself—clean every last
silver rib and feed the skin and dead-eyed head
to the mass of ants on their moving hill. Into
the small boat of those remaining bones,
fold yourself. Then row.

ACKNOWLEDGMENTS

Grateful acknowledgment to the editors of the journals in which the following poems were published, sometimes with different titles and in different form:

Big Sky Journal: "Coda"

Camas: "Bull Elk in October River"

Descant: "*Like a December apiary, the mind tapers*," "Early June, Missoula, Year of the Sheep," and "*See that my grave is swept clean*"

Hampden-Sydney Poetry Review: "The Hunt," "The Turn," and "The Congressman's Daughter"

High Desert Journal: "Lunar Calendar"

Orion: "Boy with Tree Frog"

Poetry East: "Cooking Christmas Dinner with My Son, the Runner"

Poetry Northwest: "Phrases," "Bird in My Boot", and "Dept. Meeting"

The Southern Review: "Going Home"

Southern Humanities Review: "Saying Moon in Dusk"

Talking River: "Grove"

Terrain.org: "Tablet," "Fig," and "To the First of the Getting-Longer Days"

Whitefish Review: "Just Before Dark"

Italicized titles and occasional lines are taken from lyrics by: Ketch Secor, Tom Waits, Bruce Cockburn, Mason Jennings, Joni Mitchell, Bill Monroe, Gregory Alan Isakov, Samantha Parton, Jack Ridl, Elton John, Kristian Matsson, and Willie McTell. The poet referred to in "Bird in My Boot" is of course Theodore Roethke; the poems referred to in "Little Derivative" are Melissa Kwasny's, from her exceptional collection, *The Nine Senses*; "Early June, Missoula, Year of the Sheep," refers to James and Franz Wright and borrows a line from an interview the latter gave. The nobleman quote in "The Hunt" is from Meister Eckhart. "Midwesterly" owes a line to Rossie Benasco.

Long-standing gratitude to Jim Colando, retired East Lansing High School English teacher, for tape recording and playing songs for our English classes, typed lyrics included. I must thank the wonderful songwriter Kris Delmhorst for the "death on a cracker," line, and the nonpareil Adrian Arleo for "Swallow Bust," the clay sculpture that inspired "Swallows Building Nests." "Bull Elk in October River" is for Brian Doyle, in memoriam; "Shore Song" for Dan Gerber; "Poem in Which I Lose My Wish to Drown" for Nick Popoff and Robin Fogg; "Dept. Meeting" for Mike Delp and Di Seuss; "Swale" for Mary McGinn Dombrowski, in memory of her father Joseph V. McGinn; "Tablet" for Peter and Alden Drake, with thanks to Checker Press for the limited letterpress edition, and accompanying individual watercolors by Susan Van Kampen. Thank you to James Galvin, JF, and Richard Buckner for the use of the section epigraphs.

Many people and places aided in the fashioning of these poems, and I thank them here, particularly Good Harbor, East Bay, and Square Butte, along with early manuscript readers David Duncan, Jenny Montgomery, Anne-Malin Ringwalt, and Phil Schaefer. I thank Annie Martin for her sustained belief in this collection, and the wonderful folks at WSUP for their patient, diligent stewardship. Thanks to my students at the University of Montana, Interlochen, and in the Beargrass Workshops for inspiration and courage. Thank you to my parents. I thank Jeffrey Foucault for the enduring, good light he casts on my work and life, to say nothing of the songs themselves. Finally, to those who helped usher me through a difficult phase—some aforementioned, some certainly unnoticed—I am deeply indebted. My hope is that this collection might stand however humbly as a record of deliverance, which is, to quote a late friend, never far away but often quite invisible.

ABOUT THE AUTHOR

Chris Dombrowski is the author of two previous books of poems from Wayne State University Press—*By Cold Water,* a Poetry Foundation best seller, and *Earth Again,* runner-up for *ForeWord* magazine's Book of the Year in Poetry—as well as a memoir, *Body of Water* (Milkweed Editions), a *Bloomberg News* Best Book of 2016. His poems have appeared in over a hundred anthologies and journals including *Crazyhorse, Guernica, Gulf Coast, Orion, Poetry, Poetry Northwest, The Southern Review,* and others. For the better part of two decades, he has taught creative writing to a vast array of age groups, most recently as the William Kittredge Visiting Writer-in-Residence at the University of Montana. In addition, he has worked as a fly-fishing guide in Missoula, Montana, where he directs the Beargrass Writing Workshops and makes his home with his loveably feral family.

Advance praise for *Ragged Anthem*

"'I hoped for some last gesture beyond a handshake,' writes Chris Dombrowski in *Ragged Anthem,* a soulful book of longing that is as comic as it is reflective. These poems sing of humankind in need of something it can only seem to get from the natural world, and of how we won't get it until we begin to understand ourselves as natural as any tree or river. Or as Dombrowski himself says, 'Again / I took daybreak for granted, easy / as mistaking pinecone for wasp nest, / wasp nest for shed antler, antler / for branch.' Here, these so-called mistakes make for discovery that approaches the magic of revelation."
—Jericho Brown, author of *The Tradition*

"Reading *Ragged Anthem* is like staring at the sun and then looking away. Whatever is seen next is informed and haunted by that light. Dombrowski's poems are that clear, that powerful. This book will change you."
—Kevin Goodan, author of *Anaphora*

"'It wearies one, the visionary mode,' Chris Dombrowski writes in his remarkably unweary new book of poems, *Ragged Anthem.* The anthem is ragged, to be sure, with the disillusion and tenderness that comes with age and with a closely attended wonder—at a son's words, a daughter's drawings, brook trout, swallow nest, the sound of the word *swale.* Dombrowski reminds us with the clarity of a mountain stream why poems matter."
—Melissa Kwasny, author of *Pictograph* and *Reading Novalis in Montana*

"Chris Dombrowski has proven himself to be among the best poets of his generation. As one of those readers who admired and enjoyed his first two books—better put, who has gone to the poems for spiritual sustenance, for wisdom, and for the magic of being transported to the landscapes where the poet makes his life—I'm happy to report that *Ragged Anthem* continues to sing those essential songs in beautiful and unexpected ways."
—Todd Davis, author of *Native Species* and *Winterkill*

"Chris Dombrowski's *Ragged Anthem* comes at us from the woods and the backyards of Main Street, somewhat in the tradition of Richard Hugo or B. H. Fairchild—even a more surreal version of W. C. Williams—a definite flowering in the American grain."
—Dorianne Laux, author of *Only as the Day Is Long: New and Selected Poems*

"Here, Dombrowski quotes Roethke, another Michigan treasure: 'In a dark time, the eye begins to see,' and indeed these poems *see* the turmoil and resilient beauty of contemporary America, from 'rivers strewn with moonlight and discarded / shopping carts' to 'boulder-curled cataracts / pocked by sewers.' Even weeping, here, is the beginning of the ragged anthem we desperately need."

  —Diane Seuss, author of *Still Life with Two Dead Peacocks and a Girl*
   and *Four-Legged Girl*

"There are few poets whose voices resonate with such confidence that I'd follow them from a fabricated lunar calendar to a departmental meeting to a text message—but in these gorgeous, spine-ful poems, full of the 'shrapnel of the miraculous,' I couldn't help folding over the corner on every page until the collection became as dog-eared as a pointer on a duck hunt. 'I was a creature once,' Dombrowski says, and in his poems we are allowed to return to the creatures we all once were: vital and deeply rooted in a world that is happening not on a screen or around a board room table but here and now and together. While his poems evince great skill, they are not made of artifice. Dombrowski finds the heart in the hurt thing, the burnt thing, the thing with the broken wing, the thing that doesn't know it wants to be loved until it is. And his speaker—the self-proclaimed 'poet laureate of boot slush'—vows 'to someday see / the world as the world, not a caption on my life.' It makes sense to fear for our lives in the world we live in, surrounded by our own madness and the kinds of sadnesses that are passed down from one generation to the next. But Dombrowski begs us to love each terrifying moment. And in his poems, I do. This is a book to hold close."

  —Keetje Kuipers, author of *All Its Charms*

"The magnificent poems in *Ragged Anthem* showcase Chris Dombrowski's numinous adoration of the beautiful and strange. *Ragged Anthem* is strung together from anthills and elk and geese—the text messages and decapitations that become our selves. From exquisitely reverential renderings of the natural world to the twinned experiences of love and loss, this is a superb collection, one to be savored."

  —Alex Lemon, author of *Another Last Day* and *Feverland: A Memoir*
   in Shards